The Fort

3-D Shapes

Joshua Rae Martin

Publishing Credits

Dona Herweck Rice, *Editor-in-Chief*; Lee Aucoin, *Creative Director*; Don Tran, *Print Production Manager*; Sara Johnson, *Senior Editor*; Jamey Acosta, *Associate Editor*; Neri Garcia, *Interior Layout Designer*; Stephanie Reid, *Photo Editor*; Rachelle Cracchiolo, M.A.Ed., *Publisher*

Image Credits

cover Stephanie Reid; p.1 Stephanie Reid; p.4 manley620/iStockphoto; p.5 rtguest/Shutterstock; p.6 manley620/iStockphoto; p.7 (top) Talshiar/Dreamstime, (middle) Miflippo/Dreamstime, (bottom) Carlos E. Santa Maria/Shutterstock, Angelogila/Dreamstime, Geopappas/Dreamstime, AlexAvich/Shutterstock; p.8 Monkey Business Images/Shutterstock; p.9 Fotosearch; p.10 (top) Dean Evangelista/Shutterstock, (bottom) rtguest/Shutterstock; p.11 jaroon/Shutterstock; p.12 Stephanie Reid; p.13 (top left) Indric/Shutterstock, (top right) Shcherbakov Ilya/Shutterstock, (bottom left) Icefields/Dreamstime, (bottom right) Radu Razvan/Shutterstock; p.14 (left) Alex Staroseltsev/Shutterstock, (right) Bonnie Jacobs/iStockphoto; p.15 Kvadrat/Shutterstock; p.16 (left) Microdon/Dreamstime, (right) Olivier Le Queinec/Shutterstock; p.17 (top) grynold/Shutterstock, (left) Microdon/Dreamstime, (middle left) PhotoStocker/Shutterstock, (middle right) Vadim Kozlovsky/Shutterstock, (right) Feng Yu/Shutterstock; p.18 Good Mood Photo/Shutterstock; p.19 (top) Cheryl Casey/Shutterstock, (bottom) rtguest/Shutterstock; p.20 (top left) Good Mood Photo/Shutterstock, (middle left) Anthony Berenyi/Shutterstock, (bottom left) C. Salisbury/Shutterstock, (top right) Lars Lindblad/Shutterstock, (bottom right) Elena Elisseeva/Shutterstock; p.21 (left) Carlos E. Santa Maria/Shutterstock, (middle left) Microdon/Dreamstime, (middle right) Neokan/Dreamstime, (right) prism68/Shutterstock; p.22 Stephanie Reid; p.23 Stephanie Reid; p.24 Stephanie Reid; p.25 (left) grekoff/Shutterstock, (middle) Stephanie Reid, (top right) Roman Sigaev/Shutterstock, (bottom right) Stephanie Reid; p.26 Nolie/Shutterstock; p.27 (top) Sami Haqqani.Dreamstime, (bottom) Martine Oger/Shutterstock; p.28 Tim Bradley

Teacher Created Materials

5301 Oceanus Drive
Huntington Beach, CA 92649-1030
http://www.tcmpub.com
ISBN 978-0-7439-0872-6
©2011 Teacher Created Materials, Inc.
Printed in China

Table of Contents

Boxes and Boxes

There are 8 families who live on Grant Street. One day things change a lot. The families see a moving van with traffic cones around it.

The Drake family is moving in. All the other kids watch to see what will come off the truck.

A cone has a circular **base**. The point at the other end is called a **vertex**.

vertex

base

The kids see a lot of big boxes. It sometimes helps movers to know how big a box is. You can measure the **length**, the **height**, and the **width**. Each of those measurements is called a **dimension**.

Boxes have 3 dimensions. They are called three-dimensional shapes. Another name for three-dimensional is 3–D. Some boxes are **cubes**. All the edges are equal lengths. Some boxes are rectangular prisms. The edges on those boxes have lengths that are not the same.

1.　　　2.　　　3.　　　4.

a. Which boxes are cubes?
b. Which boxes are rectangular prisms?

Helping and Having Fun

Everyone helps the new family. All the neighbors bring in boxes.

The kids want to play with the new kids. They get a great idea. They want to have fun with the boxes. They ask to keep some of them.

They play inside the boxes. Even the cat plays.

LET'S EXPLORE MATH

3-D shapes have faces. A **face** is the flat side of a 3-D shape. Look at this rectangular prism. How many faces does it have?

The young kids have fun with the boxes, too.

They make hiding places next.
They cut a window in a packing box.
The window is a rectangle.

rectangle

Rectangles and squares are 2-D shapes. They are flat and have 2 dimensions. You can measure their lengths and widths.

1.

2.

3.

4.

a. Which pictures show squares?

b. Which pictures show cubes?

c. Which pictures show both squares and cubes?

Then they use empty cans and string to make play phones. One girl talks quietly into the empty can. The other girl listens. The string carries the sound to the other can.

The cans are 3-D shapes, too. They are called **cylinders**. They have 2 faces that are shaped like circles.

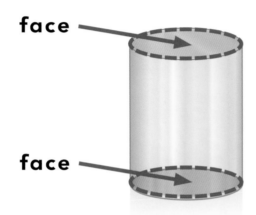

face

face

How to Make a Toy Phone

1. Remove the tops from 2 clean cans.
2. Have an adult poke a small hole in the bottom of each can.
3. Cut a piece of string at least 5 feet long. Push one end through one hole.
4. Knot it on the inside of the can. Repeat this with the other can.
5. Stretch the string tightly between the 2 cans. Talk quietly to each other.

A cylinder can be a **solid** shape.
Or it can be a **hollow** shape. A full
soup can is solid.

Take off the top of the can. Pour the soup into a bowl. Next, remove the bottom of the can. Now the cylinder is hollow.

LET'S EXPLORE MATH

1.

2.

3.

4.

a. Which pictures show hollow cylinders?

b. Which pictures show solid cylinders?

Making a Fort

The kids save a lot of boxes. They decide they want to make a fort. Then, all the kids can play together.

The Drake family used to live near a playground that looks like a fort. They have a picture of it. It gives the kids ideas.

The pointed shapes on the top of the playground are called pyramids. A pyramid has a 2-D shape as its base. Its other faces are shaped like triangles. The faces meet at a point. Just like on a cone, this point is called a vertex.

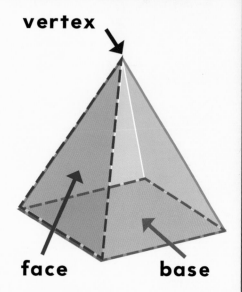

vertex

face

base

First, they make a list of the things that they can use. Then, they start to gather them together. They put the big boxes in the yard.

Things for Our Fort

1. boxes

2. cans

3. cones

4. pillows

5. blankets

6. stools

Then, they start to make the fort. They use the small boxes to build the walls.

Look at the objects below. Then answer the questions.

1.

2.

3.

4.

a. Which of these objects is shaped like a rectangular prism?

b. Which of these objects is shaped like a cube?

c. Which of these objects is shaped like a cylinder?

d. Which of these objects is shaped like a cone?

Mrs. Drake cuts a door in 1 of the big boxes. She cuts windows in 2 other big boxes.

The kids make 4 walls with boxes.
They make 1 big rectangle. They will put
cones on top of the corners later.

Having More Fun

They stack up cushions and drape a blanket to make a cozy place. They take breaks to read some books. They play in their fort all day.

That night they bring in pillows and blankets. They tell ghost stories until they have to go home for the night.

The kids on Grant Street use the fort until the weather gets cold. Then they take down the fort. They store the boxes. They start thinking about what they can make next.

All they need are some plastic boxes to pack with lots of snow to make snow bricks!

An igloo may be made of blocks of snow. The air inside the snow blocks helps keep cold weather out.

Building a Model

The Martinez family saw a picture of this playground. They wanted to make a model of it with wooden blocks. What kinds of 3-D shapes do they need to make a model?

a. How many cubes should they use?

b. How many cylinders should they use?

c. How many pyramids should they use?

d. How many ramps should they use?

e. How many rectangular prisms should they use?

Solve It!

Use the steps below to help you solve the problems.

Step 1: Look at the playground. Think about the kinds of blocks you would use to make a model. Remember that the shape would look solid in the model.

Step 2: Count the cubes for problem **a**. Count the cylinders for problem **b**.

Step 3: Count the pyramid shapes for problem **c**. Count the parts that are on a slant for problem **d**.

Step 4: Count the rectangular prisms for problem **e**. Count all the ones that you can see. Some are hidden behind the ramps. Add those to your count.

Glossary

base—the face on which a 3-D shape stands

cube—a solid shape with 6 equal sides

cylinder—a 3-D shape with 2 circular faces and 1 curved side

dimension—the length, width, or height of something

face—the flat part of a 3-D object

height—how tall something is

hollow—having empty space on the inside

length—how long something is

solid—having no empty space on the inside

vertex—a point where 2 or more edges meet

width—how wide something is

Index

Let's Explore Math

Page 7:

a. boxes 1 and 3

b. boxes 2 and 4

Page 10:

6 faces

Page 13:

a. pictures 1, 2, 3, and 4

b. pictures 3 and 4

c. pictures 3 and 4

Page 17:

a. pictures 2 and 3

b. pictures 1 and 4

Page 21:

a. object 3

b. object 1

c. object 2

d. object 4

Solve the Problem

a. 3 cubes

b. 1 cylinder

c. 1 pyramid

d. 2 ramps

e. 12 rectangular prisms